Sandra Holmes

"Shortly after the birth of my first son, Rainer, I was sitting nursing my sweet new babe and basking in the magic of the mother/babe connection when I happened to glance out the window at the farm pasture [illegible]d. All the cows had gone back up to the barn for milkin[illegible] Looking closer I noticed with [illegible]irth standing unsteady next to its [illegible] and I quickly gathered up by own n[illegible]y the time we got outside, though, th[illegible]agon to fetch the young calf. I watched [illegible]etween mother and baby, scaring back t[illegible] yelling. The baby was crying, just like my ow[illegible] too, desperately trying to get to her babe. I'll never forget t[illegible]ies. The calf was gathered up and taken up to the farm in the wagon.

I have read recently in the not milk newsletter [www.notmilk.com] how farmers are sometimes murdered by angry mother cows when they attempt to take the babies away. These normally docile creatures, so passive to give their lives for our desires, become desperate to keep their babies. Cannot we human mothers relate to this instinctual urge? When we consume dairy products we support this break of the mother/child bond. As we learn about the health concerns of dairy products it may begin to dawn on us that what is good for us is also good for our animal brothers and sisters. Dairy alternatives like almond milk offer us a bridge to a more healthy and peaceful way of life, for humans and cows."

~April Coburn, HBCE
February 2007

PRAISE FOR THE ALMOND MILK BOOK

"The Almond Milk Book by Kristin Whitcoe is a must-have for any family seeking health and wellness! This book is lively and simple! It starts with a wonderful background story about Kristin and her family and their quest for health. There are beautiful photos of her children preparing and drinking almond milk and partaking of other almond-based recipes throughout the book. You'll find clear and easy instructions for preparing nutritious and delicious almond milk along with lots of incentive to do so! Kristin provides a list of the extensive nutritional contents of almonds and traditional uses for almonds in different cultures. Included is a delightfully whimsical scripted play about almond milk that your family can enjoy reading aloud or act out yourselves just for the fun of it! With all the programming we receive from the dairy industry about the benefits of cow's milk via multi-million dollar advertising campaigns I think this play is a nice antidote and a fun way to re-orient ourselves to the benefits of this true super-food; fresh home-made almond milk made from 100% natural organic almonds!"

~ **Jinjee Talifero**, www.TheGardenDiet.com

"Kristin Whitcoe has put together an easy to use guide on Almond Milk for moms, kids, and even single men like me! Try the recipes in this book and you will discover that Almond Milk is the best milk ever!"

~ **David Wolfe**, founder of www.sunfood.com, www.thebestdayever.com, author of *The Sunfood Diet Success System, Eating For Beauty, Naked Chocolate*

"In its brilliant simplicity The Almond Milk Book is a beautiful Fairy Tale weaving together the joys of family life with the playfulness of food preparing. Making kitchen time an experience to be shared and enjoyed by everyone. A must read for children and parents alike!"

~ **Marko Eade**, www.SuccessUltraNow.com

"...I got to read your absolutely wonderful book! I just loved it!!! Great writing with lots of information even for ones, who know already about almond milk [my kids liked your recipe much better then our old one...]. Beautiful design with the artwork and so positive pictures!

~ A.W.

"I made your recipe and wow it was really delicious."

~ N.M., RN

PRAISE FOR THE ALMOND MILK BOOK

"Thank you so much for sending the lovely almond milk book. I really appreciate it. My kids just ADORE almond milk."

~ J.M.

"I love The Almond Milk Book! This is an excellent book for families with small children. Kristin shows how easy it is to make healthy delicious almond milk for your family. Children can follow the recipes and make them with mom. The play and photographs are a fabulous ways to engage and educate children on how to make almond milk and its benefits. Thanks Kristin for helping us moms."

~ **Helen Rose**, raw food mom and co-owner of
www.NaturalZing.com, raw food store

"Cool idea!!!!!! I am pregnant of my second child and looking forward to eating more raw, so I am interested in almond milk! Thank you so much for doing this!"

~ A.D.

"You have a gorgeous family and an amazing website...I honor you for going out of your way to spread the glorious message about raw food and health.... Your message is a vital one and the gift you give the world is priceless! Thank you for your tremendous contribution. You're a giver of love and light, even looking at your photos of you and your family, there's so much radiance in all of your eyes!"

~ Dina M. El-Maddah

"Almond milk has become a near ritual in our family. One of the last things we do before going to bed is make sure there are almonds soaking for the morning. Making the almond milk is a regular part of the "morning stuff" my husband does (in addition to taking out the compost, making wheat grass juice and vegetable juice, and feeding our dog Rilee). As soon as the almond milk is made it becomes a base for a creamy and delicious green smoothie which starts off every day for our son Rainer (4 years). The rest goes into the fridge to be reached for throughout the day for drinks and recipes. This creamy and simple recipe is such a gift from nature.

In The Almond Milk Book my dear friend Kristin shares this gift with you. It is truly a celebration of the gifts this simple and nourishing food has given to her family". **"A joy to read!"**

~ April Coburn

THE ALMOND MILK BOOK

Kristin Whitcoe
With Calvin, Cosette, and Kurt Whitcoe

www.TheAlmondMilkBook.com

Published by The Almond Milk Book
PO Box 701
Patagonia, AZ 85624

ISBN-13: 978-0-9794837-2-1
ISBN-10: 0-9794837-2-7

The content & cover art for this book is provided by the author Kristin Whitcoe unless otherwise documented within the pages of the book. The cover design is by Chris Whitcoe. The layout and design of the book by Nathan Holaway.

For additional copies of this book and for more information, contact the author through the website: **www.TheAlmondMilkBook.com**

Note: This book offers information based on my personal experiences. It is meant to be a guide to expand your knowledge base and pursuits, and it is not a prescription for your health or wellness. For best, better, and worse, you are solely responsible for outcomes to your life in relation to this book.

DEDICATION

This book is dedicated to Chris.

Thank you for the gift of your charm, enthusiasm, gentle strength, loving heart, purposeful sense, visions, wisdom, compassion for all people, and parenting our beautiful children together. I am grateful for becoming friends in our college days. You always bring out the best in me and keep me reaching for my highest potential. It is one of my greatest delights to experience the abundance of life with you.

To our children ~ Calvin, Cosette, and Kurt who have made this book as real as it gets. You are Earth angels and my guiding lights.

To Brad ~ Thank you for enlightening me with your smile and indigo radiance, for your enduring encouragement, and for reviving the game of baseball in my life – reminding me of the truth: “If you build it, they will come.”

CONTENTS

INTRODUCTION

If ever there is a food that receives so much attention today, it is milk. From our earliest days, just after birth, the nourishment we get from food comes to us through milk—be it human mother's milk, cow's milk-based and soy milk-based formulas, or sometimes another milk such as goat's milk.

We place a great deal of emphasis on the importance of milk. So often when breast-fed and formula-fed children have been weaned from their initial milk sources, many continue to receive a substantial part of their life's nutrition through milk. In my culture, this has meant cow's milk. A large percentage of people I know continue drinking cow's milk throughout their adult lives too. Even if they drink little cow's milk or none at all, dairy is a significant source of nutrition for them, with cheese, yogurt, and ice cream as popular choices.

In the past few years, I received a copy of Robert Cohen's book Milk A-Z. In it he cites numerous research studies which dismantle the importance of cow's milk and dairy as critical needs in our diets. In fact, his work reveals alarming correlations between cow's milk and disease in people. While I have not outlined specific research in this book to support evidence that cow's milk and dairy is bad for human consumption, my own personal experiences and encounters with everyday people is enough for me to look for an alternative to cow's milk and dairy products. It is a reason to give cow's milk back to the cows. And it is an incentive to bring cows and people back to the land, and out of offensive farms and factories.

Headaches, earaches and ear infections, recurring colds and runny noses, sore throats, coughs and asthma, eczema, constipation and bloating are few of the ongoing problems I find people experiencing in relation to cow's milk and dairy consumption. These symptoms might seem commonplace, but for people who rarely and never have such nagging and debilitating issues, they are unnecessary. These conditions take away from the zest of life and they interfere with day-to-day living. To be around people who have such symptoms time after time is uninspiring.

A year-and-a-half ago, my neighbor borrowed Cohen's book from me in a conscious effort to deal with her son's chronic asthma. Instantly after reading the book, her family decided to give up cow's milk. Nearly as instantaneous, her son's asthma subsided and vanished. My neighbor expressed deepest gratitude for such a simple remedy: give up cow's milk.

If not cow's milk and dairy products, then what? Many people who follow vegetarian and vegan diets already are well-versed in commercially-packaged choices such as soymilk, rice milk, almond milk, and oat milk. I think these options are much better for us and for the sustainability of our planet.

While the primary message of this book is to support you in giving up cow's milk and dairy, I am equally in favor of promoting plant-based nut and seed milks from nuts and seeds organically grown and kept in their raw, living states. Again, while I have no revealing research contained in this book, proof in personal encounters overwhelmingly supports the raw food option.

Our family has found the goodness of milk through almonds. This book is based on our transition from cow's milk to homemade raw organic almond milk and adopting a diet with significant amounts of raw, living, organic, and vegan foods. It is my deepest wish that you, the reader, finds a glimmer of truth within the pages of this book—for yourself, for your loved ones, and perhaps for your neighbor down the street.

Included in this book is our family's recipe for homemade raw organic almond milk. I hope you enjoy making it, sharing the experience with others, and coming up with your own special blends. With little effort, homemade raw organic almond milk—and raw organic almonds and raw organic almond butter—is an easy way to add vitality to your life in a manner that is also economical, and a contributing factor to Earth sustainability.

Art by Calvin (2007)

WHY DRINK HOMEMADE RAW ORGANIC ALMOND MILK?

- It tastes good.
- It is fun to make.
- It is fun to share.
- It is economical.
- It is pure.
- It is natural.
- It is refreshing.
- It is hydrating.
- It is easy to make.
- Kids like it.
- Kids can make it.
- Moms like it.
- Dads like it.
- Grandmothers like it.
- Everybody likes it.
- Everybody can make it.
- It offers variety.
- It has life-force.
- It is a raw food.
- It is energizing.
- It is not pasteurized.
- It makes great smoothies.
- It gives milk back to the cows.
- It doesn't come from a cow.
- It is vegetarian.
- It is vegan.
- It is more resourceful for our environment.
- It supports organic farmers.
- It is packed with vitamins and minerals.
- It is a nutritional boost.
- It is not part of soy controversy.
- It contains no harmful additives.
- It is basic health insurance.
- People will want to know your secret.
- It comes from an almond.

What can you do with 52 pounds of raw, organic almonds?

Make homemade raw organic almond milk everyday and save money through bulk purchases!

OUR STORY

From the time I entered the world, I started drinking a cow's milk-based formula. When I finished the bottle, I started drinking cow's milk. I drank lots and lots of cow's milk for nearly 2 _ decades. I didn't drink it straight up in the morning, but had it in my breakfast cereal and warm oatmeal. Faithfully, I drank a glass of milk with lunch and dinner, and often with a snack. Regularly I held the cold gallon carton from store to home. Cold milk was a cosmic beverage. Equally as pleasing to me: milk-dunking crunchy cookies and graham crackers, thereby transforming them into soft and sweeter selections.

I had my fill of other sources of dairy, too. Fruity yogurt, hunks of cheese with crackers, cookies & cream and peanut butter cup ice creams, and cottage cheese with applesauce were some of my dairy delights of choice. As years of my childhood passed, I became well-versed in words like whole, 2 percent, 1 percent, and skim. Going from the whole milk fat to the skim variety was a big change. One year on a hot summer day while breaking from college studies, I babysat for a six year-old girl who liked milk probably as much as me. I remember one afternoon I prepared to wash her unfinished glass of whole milk and the milk literally fell out of the glass in a solid mass with a most peculiar smell. Nonetheless, I adjusted and I stuck to dairy…like it stuck to me as I would find out years later.

I married in 1998 and my husband Chris and I drank milk together. We had our first child one year later. I breastfed our son while I continued consuming milk. My husband and I went organic when we began to feed our son foods other than mother's milk. We learned about organic milk, buying it by the cartons and then the bottles. Once, I even volunteered at our local food co-op to pick up the farm milk in bottles and bring them back to the store. I was disappointed when the farm owners sold their business.

By this time, however, I was starting to question my cow's milk and dairy consumption. Something about me didn't feel quite right. I remembered having an ongoing cold or stuffy nose ever since I was about 7 years old. Medical professionals diagnosed the symptom as seasonal allergies. Along with nose irritation, I experienced itchy eyes, sore throat, wheezing and coughing, and headaches.

Even before I had these symptoms, I encountered numerous ear infections as a child. My stomach ached often, and I complained of abdominal bloating and bowel constipation. At age 12, my tonsils and adenoids were removed by surgery. Later I had trouble staying focused in school during my menstrual periods. I went home early one day as the pain was ultimately unbearable.

An avid runner in my high school days with moments of ranking glory, running became increasingly difficult as I developed sharp abdominal pains that coursed through my legs, leaving me with dull, throbbing aches, and a quitter's mentality. I medicated multitudes of discomforts with prescribed medication, including pills for allergies, inhalers for asthma, pink stuff for stomach aches, more pills for menstrual cramps, and white tablets for headaches. Even with a panel of pills, my symptoms escalated when I encountered cats, cigarette smoke, freshly cut grass, and dust.

While pregnant with our first child, I took a more discerning approach to medication. Even prior to pregnancy, I was cautious about medication use, and didn't like taking it very often. However, while pregnant, I was reluctant to use any, and considered that by taking medications I might adversely affect our unborn baby.

My symptoms persisted. So did my daily dairy intake, probably more so. On one of my pregnant nights after Chris and I had been in bed for awhile with lights out, I innocently asked him to get me a snack of cheese and crackers. Sometime between our first child's first year and my third pregnancy, I learned about other types of non-dairy milk. The first being soymilk. Incidentally, I had a close encounter with soymilk during my first pregnancy. One day Chris bought some for me to drink, and after one sip I politely positioned the box in the refrigerator, eventually pouring it down the kitchen sink drain. I didn't revisit soymilk until a year or two later.

With a little research and through casual conversations, I started to believe my extensive ailments were related to cow's milk and dairy consumption. Once again, I rediscovered soymilk. It became forefront in our fridge. What pleased my palate this time was the vanilla variety, simply smooth and slightly sweet. We served it to our children. We bought it by the case.

Instead of having cow's milk and cereal, I relished morning breakfasts of soymilk and cereal. Over a short period of time, I noticed a subtle reduction in symptoms. One revelation was feeling lighter and less bloated after breakfast, and with increased clarity and energy. A simple equation for me: the less dairy I consumed, the less symptoms I suffered.

Again, a growing concern for me was data I started to receive about side effects of over-consumption of soymilk. Various sources indicated that not only cow's milk might be linked to illness and disease, but soymilk might as well. Our next approach was to bring rice milk home. It offered a similar smooth and sweet sensation and gave me more peace of mind as I believed it was a healthier option for Chris, our two children, and our one unborn baby.

I wasn't completely at ease with our rice milk ritual. During this time, we briefly explored local raw cow's milk, and sometimes sipped boxed almond milk. I even tried to make almond milk based on a recipe I found. The results weren't too tasty, and I used a lot of almonds and incurred higher food bills. In the end, we preferred rice milk. But upon reading the box label again and again, I wondered how much substantial nutrients it offered.

Coinciding with these experiences was a catalyst for a significant transformation in our overall health and well-being. In early 2003, while six months pregnant with our third child, my dear friend introduced me to raw foods. It started in her kitchen over packaged dehydrated chips, crackers, and cookies. I was so intrigued by this concept, the scrumptious snacks, and my friend's new cookbook, or no-cook book, that is. I went home and by evening I had my own copy of this book, ready to relish the recipes.

Instantly I believed whole-heartedly that raw foods would support my health tremendously. Because I was pregnant, I considered carefully how to introduce them into my daily nutrition, so as to maximize benefits without compromising my pregnancy by way of radical changes to my current-at-the-time cuisine. Each day I widened my repertoire of raw food recipes. One of the first Chris and I enjoyed was the raw vegan ice cream. Made with pine nuts (a first-time taste), dates, and touch of vanilla, we made a meal out of dessert. Soon we learned the amount of raw foods we would consume would be less than the amount of food we classified as cooked, due to the density of nutrients in the raw food.

In these early days of our raw food experiences, I revived almond milk-making. I made milks with other nuts and seeds too: Brazil nuts, cashews, hemp nuts, pecans, walnuts, pumpkin seeds, sesame seeds, and sunflower seeds. Aside from my mother's milk that nourished our babies, these nuts and seeds became the source of milk in the family.

In a relatively short period of time my senses shifted to see the vast value of plant-based milk sources while that fascination with cow's milk and dairy faded away. With passing years, I cultivate more personal experiences in praise of plant-based nutrition. My distressing symptoms of yesterday are gone.

I continue to study current research, comparing dairy and plant-based nutrition (including nuts and seeds, fruits, greens, land and sea vegetables, and "super foods"), and I'm extensively in favor of plant-based provisions. Fresh, homemade nut and seed milks are staples in our home. I continue to meet countless others who radiate health, wellness, and beauty from the bounty of raw, living, plant-based foods.

Art by Cosette (2007)

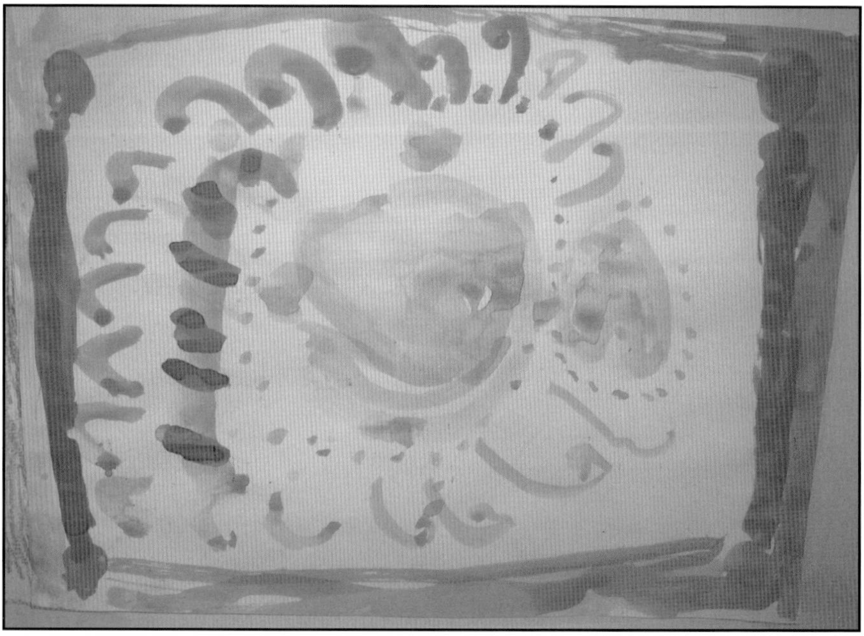

Art by Cosette (2007)

POEM

A is for almond
Really good to eat
It's a nut from a tree
Nutritious and a treat

Almonds for a snack
Can be roasted or raw
Raw ones soaked in water
Sprout new life for all

Calcium and potassium
Magnesium and phosphorus
Plus packed with protein
Almonds are really good for us

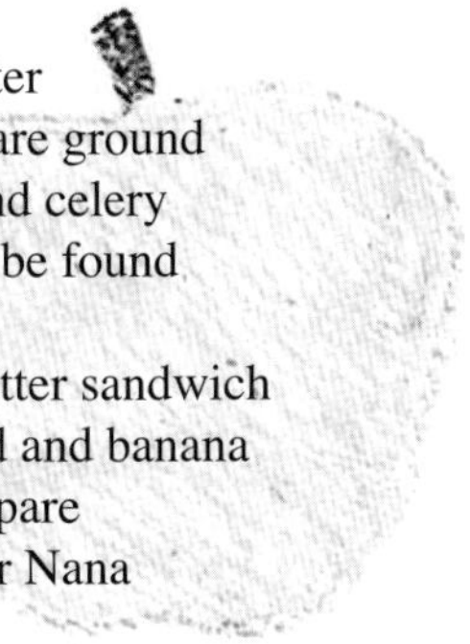

A is for almond butter
When the almonds are ground
Taste with apples and celery
Here's a treasure to be found

Make an almond butter sandwich
With sprouted bread and banana
Fun and easy to prepare
And share with your Nana

A spoonful of almond butter
Blended in a favorite drink
Delightful any time of day
So simply smooth you'll think

A is for almond milk
A drink made from the nut
You can buy it in a food store
Or make some in your hut

With almonds, nut milk, and more
Please buy organic
These food and drinks are handled with care
And healing for our planet

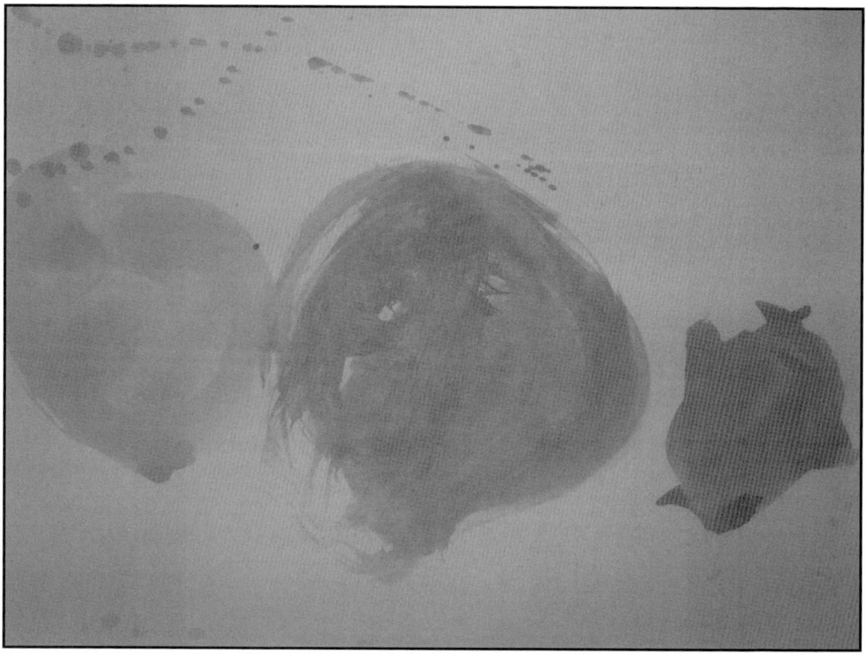

Art by Cosette (2007)

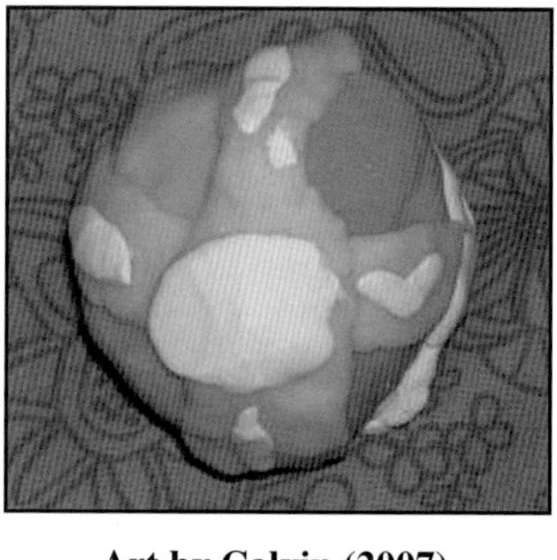

Art by Calvin (2007)

HOMEMADE RAW ORGANIC ALMOND MILK RECIPE

Whether you are a child, parent, or grandparent, younger or older, you can prepare raw almond milk in your own kitchen!

Step 1 of 4:

Gather these ingredients [found in "organic" or "natural foods" section of large grocery stores, in natural food stores far and wide, and through internet retail stores]:

Raw Almonds
Drinking water
Celtic Sea or Himalayan Crystal Salt
Cinnamon or
Nutmeg or
Pumpkin Pie Spice
Dried Dates or
Raw Honey or
Agave Nectar or
Stevia extract

Shop for organic ingredients as health insurance and as a measure to protect and care for our environment. Unsprayed and pesticide-free almonds are often available if organic ones are not. Use clean, bottled, filtered, and/or collected-from-a-fresh-spring-source water that is free from chlorine and other toxic contaminants. The type of salt does matter: Celtic Sea Salt and Himalayan Crystal Salt are found naturally on the planet. They contain an abundance of health-supporting minerals and when used moderately they seem to help the body balance unlike ordinary table salt which has been highly processed. Raw honey tastes different than cooked honey. Most often it is rather solid compared to its more liquid counterpart. Raw honey can be scooped from the jar with a spoon, and contains a layer of pollen, propolis, and beeswax, offering beneficial minerals, vitamins, enzymes, amino acids, and carbohydrates.

Step 2 of 4:

- **Soak 1 Cup [1C] of Raw Almonds in water in a jar overnight in the refrigerator.**
- **1C raw almonds = about 2C soaked almonds**
- **In the morning, drain soaking water from jar and rinse almonds.**
- **Place 2C soaked almonds in blender container.**
- **Fill container with drinking water to 8C line.**

Note—any blender will make almond milk, though a more powerful blender will produce the smoothest almond milk in less time. We use the Vita-Prep blender by VitaMix.®

Step 3 of 4:

- **Blend almonds and water for about 1-3 minutes.**
- **Transfer blend to another pitcher.**
- **Place strainer or mesh bag over blender container.**
- **Pour mixture from pitcher over strainer in blender container to separate almond pulp from milk.**
- **Set pulp aside to use in another recipe or to compost.**

Step 4 of 4:

- **Flavor almond milk with 1 teaspoon of Sea Salt per 8C almond milk and 1/2 teaspoon Cinnamon or Nutmeg or Pumpkin Pie Spice.**

- **Sweeten almond milk with 8 Dried Dates, pits removed OR 4-5 Tablespoons Honey OR 4-5 Tablespoons Agave Nectar OR 30 drops Stevia extract.**

* **Also, try blending in 1C Raisins, soaked in water for 1 hour [use the water for this recipe or another].**

Note—for a bonus boost of nutrients, I often add 1Tablespoon or more of flax, olive, or hemp oils to 8C of prepared almond milk. These oils contain necessary fat and essential fatty acids (omegas).

This delicious almond milk is now ready to drink and share with friends! Fresh almond milk will last 2-3 days when chilled & sealed tight from air.

Food for thought—what are reasons one drinks cow's milk? Is it for the Fat? Protein? Vitamin D? Calcium? Taste? Does cow's milk really offer these benefits and does it really support a healthy body? We are the only species on the planet that regularly and willingly consumes the milk of another species. We are the only species on the planet that consumes milk of any type long after infancy into our adult lives. Is this behavior in line with the rest of nature, and with other mammals? Could fresh, home-made almond milk be the perfect substitute for cow's milk? Complete with nutrients and flavor to support excellent health and well-being?

Photo & almond milk by Calvin (2007)

"Almonds and Chestnuts"

Pat-a-cake, pat-a-cake, cookies for sale,
Almonds and chestnuts and figs in a pail.
Cinnamon, marshmallow, strawberry treat-
Mommy makes cookies for somebody sweet.

-Pio Peep! Traditional Spanish Nursery Rhymes
By Alma Flor Ada and F. Isabel Campoy
English adaptions by Alice Schertle

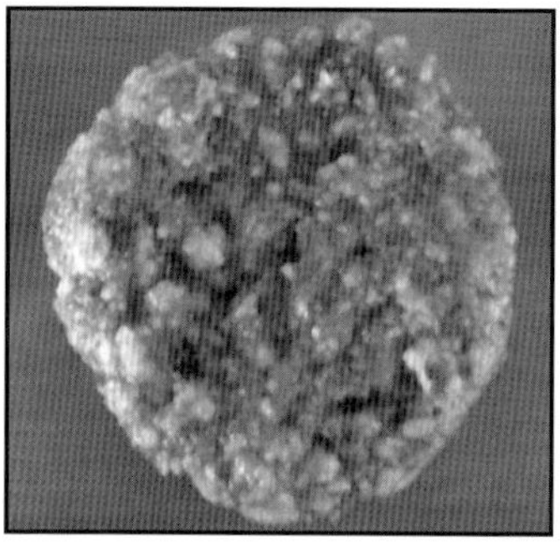

Cookie Recipe, page 31

"Cookies" by Cosette (2006)

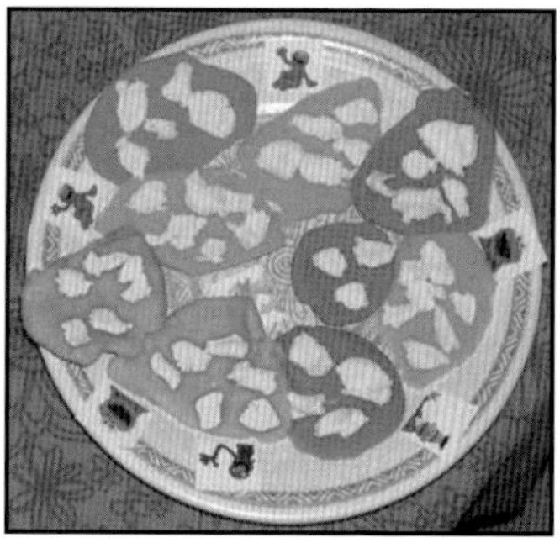

HOMEMADE RAW ORGANIC ALMOND MILK PHOTOS

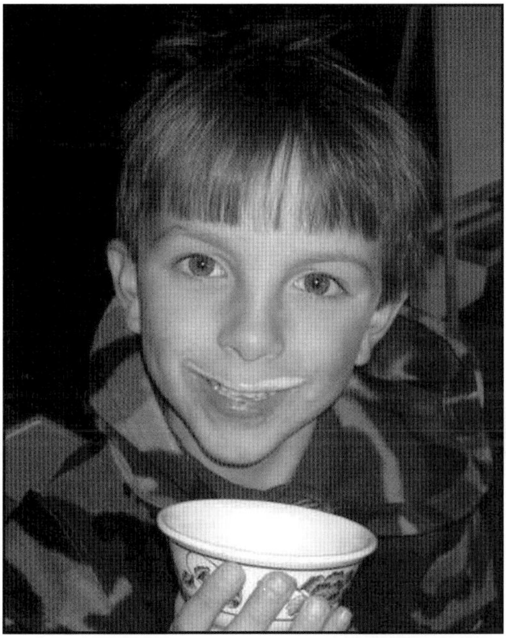

Calvin "almond milk smile"

Raw, dry almonds

Raw, soaked (overnight) almonds

Cosette (5) with basket of soaked almonds

Kurt (3) milks almonds

Calvin (7) milks almonds

Cosette "one teaspoon" nose

Cosette measures agave nectar

Kurt sips almond milk

Calvin and Kurt measure agave nectar

Cup of fresh, homemade almond milk

Calvin sips almond milk

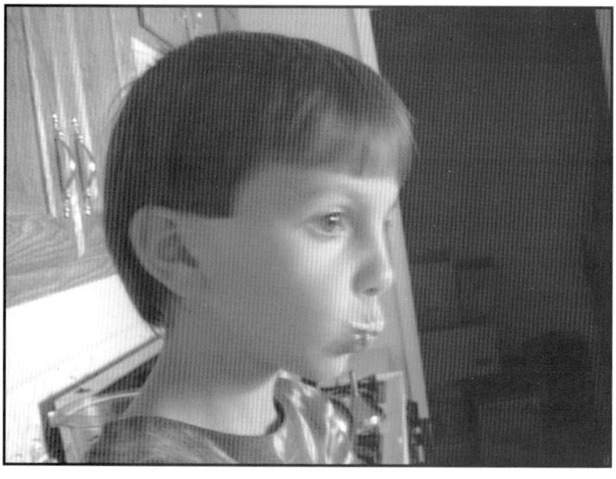

"Almond milk moustache"

Cosette poses with almond milk

Kurt drinks almond milk

MORE RECIPES & PHOTOS

1. ABC SMOOTHIE

Blend together:

1C	Almond Milk (see Raw Almond Milk Recipe)
1	Organic Banana
1T	Raw Carob or Raw Chocolate Powder

Note—raw carob powder is a fun, useful ingredient to have on hand. It has a rich taste which resembles chocolate and might be a substitute to chocolate for those who consider raw chocolate to be over-stimulating. Carob powder, made from the carob pod that grows on trees, also tastes sweet, compared to pure raw chocolate which is stronger on the palate. Both are enjoyable ingredients with many values. Depending upon one's philosophy, this smoothie might be a "light chocolate" or "dark chocolate" blend!

---

2. APPLES & RAW ALMOND BUTTER

Eat together:
A colorful variety of local, organic apple chunks dipped in a bowl of raw, organic almond butter

Apples and Homemade Raw Almond Butter

3. RAW ALMONDS

Set raw almonds in a bowl and eat one-by-one.
Take delight in peeling off the skins (of soaked almonds) if you wish!

---

4. EASY RAW ORGANIC ALMOND MILK

Blend together:

1C	Water
2T	Raw Organic Almond Butter
Pinch	Salt
1/2T	Agave nectar or Local, Raw Honey

---

5. COOKIES-FOR-BREAKFAST

Blend or process & shape into cookies on a plate:

1C	Raw, organic almonds
1C	Organic Raisins
1/2C	Coconut Butter
1	Organic Apple (cut into pieces)
Pinch	All-Spice
Pinch	Himalayan Crystal Salt or Celtic Sea Salt

Chill for 20-30 minutes – if you can wait – they go fast!

---

6. RAW ALMONDS & RAISINS

Scoop a handful of dry and/or soaked raw almonds and a handful of organic raisins into a bag or take-a-long container and snack-on-the way!

Almonds & Monukka Raisins

7. SO-SMOOTH -YOU'LL-LOVE ARUGULA-ALMOND MILK SMOOTHIE

Blend together:

4C	Almond Milk (see Raw Almond Milk Recipe)
1	Small Organic Avocado
1	Large Handful of Organic [Local] Arugula

---

8. COOL & CREAMY CAULIFLOWER WITH FRESH & CRUNCHY RAW ALMOND BUTTER DRESSING

Blend or process florets of 1 organic Cauliflower until smooth & creamy, and place in a serving bowl.

Blend or process together Dressing:

1/2C	Raw Almonds
4T	Olive Oil
4T	Apple Cider Vinegar
4T	Water
2	Small handfuls of Parsley greens
1-2 tsp	Himalayan Crystal (or Celtic Sea) Salt
1 pinch	Cumin
1 pinch	Chili Powder

Add dressing to the bowl with cauliflower, stir, and serve!
Eat as is, or accompany with red pepper slices, lettuce leaves, and celery sticks.
Try topped with a sprinkling of dulse flakes.

---

9. RAW ALMOND BUTTER & BANANA ON BREAD OR SANDWICH

Spread raw almond butter on one slice of sprouted grain bread.
Slice one organic banana and top on another slice of sprouted grain bread.
Sprinkle cinnamon on banana slices if you wish.
Make a sandwich, or eat one slice at a time, or alternate bites from one slice of bread to another!

Cosette with almond butter & banana on sprouted cinnamon raisin bread

Almond butter & bananas

Calvin with almond butter & banana on sprouted cinnamon raisin bread

---

10. CAROB GINGER PUDDING

Blend or process:

1/2 inch	Fresh Organic Ginger
1/2C	Raw Organic Walnuts

Add:

1C	Almond Milk Pulp (the leftover part of the milk)
1C	Raw Carob Powder
1/2C	Water
1-2T	Local, Raw Honey

Blend or process all ingredients until smooth, light, and fluffy. Eat it with a spoon. Dip in apple slices too!

Carob Ginger Pudding

11. HOMEMADE RAW ALMOND BUTTER

Blend together until creamy:

1C Dry (or Soaked & Dried) Raw Almonds
2T Cold-Pressed Olive Oil or Coconut Butter
1/2 tsp Himalayan Crystal Salt (or Celtic Sea Salt)
1T Local, Raw Honey

Note—the VitaMix® blender is useful for this recipe.

---

12. KRISTIN'S FAVORITE RAW ALMOND MILK SUPER SMOOTHIE

Blend together:

7C Almond Milk (see Raw Almond Milk Recipe)
1T Raw Carob Powder
1T Raw Chocolate Powder
Handful Local Organic Greens

Note—try also another blend with superfoods Maca, Mesquite Meal and Spirulina.

---

13. SPECIAL BREAKFAST

Pour homemade raw almond milk over a mixed bowl of walnuts, pecans, sunflower and pumpkin seeds, shredded coconut, raisins, and chopped apples, with a sprinkling of nutmeg, spirulina, and organic rolled oats.

Special Breakfast with homemade raw organic almond milk

14. COSETTE'S CUP OF WARM CHOCOLATE

Blend together:

1C	Almond Milk (see Raw Almond Milk Recipe)
1tsp	Raw Carob Powder
1tsp	Raw Chocolate Powder
1tsp	Local, Raw Honey
2C	Hot Tea (We used Yogi Tea® Vanilla Hazelnut.)

---

15. CALVIN'S HOT CHOCOLATE

Mix together:

1C	Hot Water
1tsp	Local, Raw Honey
2T	Raw Carob Powder

Sprinkling of Allspice

---

16. SUNNY-ANY-DAY-PIZZA-ON-A-PLATE

For the crust, process and press onto a dinner plate:

1C	Soaked Raw Organic Almonds
1C	Organic Carrot
1/2C	Almond Milk Pulp
1/4C	Cold-pressed Olive Oil
Pinch	Himalayan Crystal Salt (or Celtic Sea Salt)

For the sauce:
Soak in water and blend sun-dried tomatoes into a sauce. Spread as much a layer as you wish onto the crust.

For the topping, mix together and spread onto pizza crust:

2T	Raw Organic Tahini (Sesame Seed Butter)
1	Orange, juiced

Sprinkling of dried pizza seasoning herbs, or fresh ones if you have them!

Note—also try a crust with ground flax seeds and dehydrate the crust if you have the equipment and make the time and effort.

17. COSETTE'S RAISIN CHOCOLATE CAKE

Mix together and spread in a dish:
Almond Milk Pulp
Local, Raw Honey
Raw Carob Powder

Decorate with:
Organic Raisins
Goji Berries
Coconut Butter (She used Artisana® brand.)

Keep in freezer for an "ice cream cake" consistency.

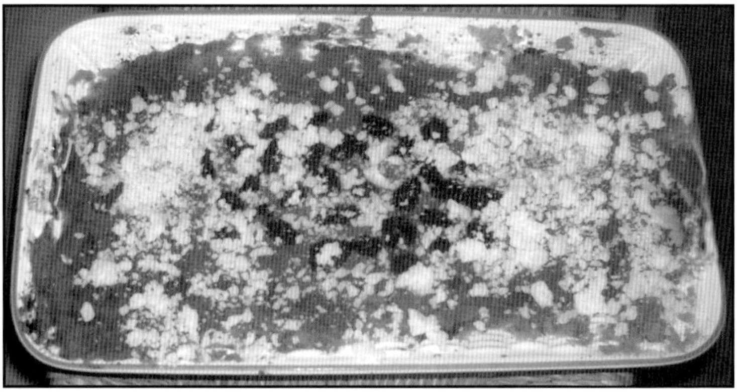

Cosette's Raisin Chocolate Cake

---

18. BIG COOKIE

Place all ingredients in a blender of food processor and blend until the mix is a thick paste and ingredients are mostly processed [some bits may remain]:

1C	Soaked Raw Organic Almonds
1/2C	Goji Berries
1/2C	Raw Carob Powder
4T	Dark Agave Nectar
1T	Raw, Organic Coconut Butter
1T	Raw, Organic Coconut Oil

Spread mix onto a plate and shape into a cookie. Cosette suggests molding the edges as one might do with a pie or pizza crust, and slicing apples to decorate the top and enjoy with each bite.

Chill for a more dense serving sensation. Also try with raisins in the blend!

Big Cookie

19. WILD GREEN ALMOND MILK

Blend together:
8C Homemade, Raw, Organic Almond Milk
1C Lambsquarter or available & preferred Wild, Edible Greens
1T Spirulina

Blend in ice for a chilled & refreshing smoothie.

---

20. CREAMY CAULIFLOWER & ALMOND SAUCE

Blend or process:
1/2 Head of Organic Cauliflower, chopped
3/4C Soaked Raw, Organic Almonds
1/2C Olive Oil
1/4C Water
2T Dijon Mustard
1tsp Salt
1/2tsp Cumin
2 dashes Curry Powder
1tsp Prepared Hot Sauce

Mix into 3 spiral-sliced (resembling long pasta noodles) Zucchini & serve.

21. CHIA PUDDING WITH ALMOND MILK PULP

Soak 1/2C Chia Seeds in water for about 10 minutes until seeds have soaked up water.

Blend or process until smooth and creamy:

4 Small Organic Mangoes (cut into small pieces & skins removed [or leave on skins if you prefer this taste!])
5 Organic Coconut Date Rolls (available for bulk purchase in most natural food stores)
1/2C Almond Milk Pulp (the pulp remaining when making almond milk)
Soaked Chia Seeds

---

22. A NUT LOAF

Process:

2C	Raw, Organic Almonds (soaked overnight)
2C	Raw, Organic Pumpkin Seeds (soaked overnight)
1C	Raw, Organic Chia Seeds
2C	Organic Sundried Tomatoes (soaked in water overnight to rehydrate - save water for recipe)
3	Cloves Organic Garlic

Mix in:

1	Small Organic Red Onion, chopped
1	Bunch Cilantro, chopped
1tsp	each of Sea (or Crystal) Salt, Cinnamon, Ground Cumin, Curry Powder
1T	Dried Thyme
1T	Raw Carob Powder

Mix well all of the ingredients. Shape mixture into loaf-sized portions. Serve right away or chill until meal time. If you have a dehydrator, add some of the sundried tomato soak water into the mix before shaping into loaves. Dehydrate for the day or overnight.

Note - try using a juicer with the blank plate for processing. Grated Zucchini adds a nice texture and flavor in the mix too.

A PLAY

The setting for this play takes place at home in a cozy, small Southwestern USA town. The sun is shining, the birds are singing, and the day time temperature is warm and welcoming. Through 3 scenes, one family discovers almonds and the joy of almond milk. The characters, in order of appearance, include Apple (the oldest son), Amandine (the mother), Banana (the grandmother who is visiting), Strawberry (the daughter), Cashew (the youngest son), Fig (the father), and Coconut (the grandfather who is mentioned). They are staged in 2 rooms of the home: the kitchen & the living room—open air to the kitchen.

ACT ONE - SCENE 1

Amandine is in the kitchen. Fig is working at the computer in the living room. Banana is at the kitchen table shopping for curtains through home catalogs. Apple enters the kitchen. Strawberry and Cashew are playing outside.

Apple: Hi Mom! I just built the best fort ever. I'm hungry! What are you making?

Amandine: I'm making sandwiches. Would you like one?

Apple: Yea! Peanut butter & jelly is my favorite!

Amandine: Actually, Apple, this is an *almond butter* & jelly sandwich.

Apple: Almond *what-er?*

Banana: Don't almonds come from weddings?

Amandine: Actually, Mom, you're right. The traditional wedding favor of 5 Jordan almonds originated in Italy in the 1350s. They symbolize the 5 qualities of a happy marriage: health, wealth, happiness, fertility, and longevity.*

Apple: You mean if I eat a lot of almonds I can have a lot of money?

Amandine: Well, this almond butter & jelly sandwich is a great start. Enjoy your sandwich Apple. And please take one outside to Strawberry and Cashew.

ACT ONE - SCENE 2

Amandine is in the kitchen. Fig is working at the computer in the living room.

Banana is at the kitchen table shopping for curtains through home catalogs. Strawberry enters the kitchen. Apple and Cashew are outside.

Amandine: Strawberry would like to help me prepare a snack?

Strawberry: Yes, Mom! What are we going to eat?

Amandine: Apples & almond butter.

Banana: Almonds & apple butter?

Amandine: That's a great idea, too, Mom!

Strawberry: For now, I'll cut the apples. We can eat them plain or dipped in almond butter.

Amandine: Thank you, Strawberry. Here's the knife and cutting board. Be careful with the knife.

ACT ONE - SCENE 3

Amandine is in the kitchen. Fig is working at the computer in the living room. Banana is at the kitchen table shopping for curtains through home catalogs. Apple, Strawberry, and Cashew are outside.

Fig: Amandine, I'm hungry. What can I have for a snack?

Amandine: Here is a bowl of almonds for you.

Fig: We've been having a lot of almonds lately. I thought the saying was "an apple a day." How can one make it on almonds?

Amandine: Fig, did you know that in The Bible's Book of Genesis, Jacob sent his sons to Egypt to ask for help during famine. Bearing almonds as a gift, they were able to win the Egyptian overseer's favor.*

Banana: Does this mean I'm getting almonds for Christmas?

ACT TWO - SCENE 1

Amandine is in the kitchen. Fig is working at the computer in the living room. Banana is at the kitchen table shopping for curtains through home catalogs. Apple & Strawberry enter the kitchen. Cashew is napping.

Apple: I'm thirsty Mom. What can I have to drink?

Amandine: How about some water?

Apple: I've already had a lot of water to drink today. I want something else.

Amandine: Would you like to try this almond milk?

Banana: *Almond* milk? I thought milk came from cows.

Amandine: Yes, Mom, milk does come from cows, as well as other sources. Baby cows drink their mother's milk. And many people drink mother cow's milk too, fresh from the farm or from containers sold in stores.

Strawberry: Didn't I use to drink mother's milk?

Amandine: Yes, and so did Apple and Cashew…human mother's milk that is.

ACT TWO - SCENE 2

Amandine & Cashew are in the kitchen. Fig is working at the computer in the living room. Banana & Strawberry are at the kitchen table shopping for curtains through home catalogs. Apple enters the kitchen.

Cashew: More almond milk please!

Amandine: I'm so glad you like it, Cashew.

Apple: Mom, I'm thirsty. Do you have anymore of that almond milk?

Amandine: No, I'm sorry. Cashew & I finished the last bit. Good news, though, I'm going to make some more.

Fig: Amandine, *first* it was almond butter. *Then* it was almonds. I thought it was a bit odd you brought home almond milk for us to drink too. Now you tell us you're going to *make* almond *milk?* What about good nutrition…calcium, protein, magnesium & potassium...things like that?

Amandine: I'm glad you asked, Fig. Almonds have calcium, and are packed with vitamin E, magnesium, protein, potassium. They are low in saturated fat, high in fiber, and have no cholesterol. The USDA suggests a serving of about 23 almonds or 1 ounce a day.* So if water is the "fountain of youth," wouldn't a drink made of almonds and water be *great* nutrition?

Fig: Hmmm, interesting.

Banana: Potassium doesn't just come from a pill.

ACT TWO - SCENE 3

Fig, Apple & Strawberry are in the kitchen. Amandine is working at the computer in the living room. Banana & Cashew are at the kitchen table shopping for curtains through home catalogs.

Fig: Amandine, have you seen the olive oil?

Amandine: I'm sorry; Fig, but we finished it with last night's dinner.

Fig: How am I supposed to make my special salad dressing?

Amandine: Try using some almond butter.

Apple: Yeah, Dad, let's invent a new special dressing like other people do in recipe books.

Strawberry: I'll stir it up!

Banana: Do almonds grow on trees?

Amandine: Yes, Mom, almonds do grow on trees. Nearly 500 miles of California almond orchards produce over 80% of the world's supply of almonds. And compared with olive oil, almond butter contains more protein, fiber, calcium, iron, magnesium, phosphorous, zinc, manganese, niacin, folate, vitamin E, & more amino acids—the building blocks of protein. In addition, it has fewer calories, less fat & saturated fatty acids.*

Cashew: Please may I lick the spoon?

Strawberry: Let's take a trip to California!

ACT THREE - SCENE 1

Amandine is in the kitchen. Fig is working at the computer in the living room. Banana is at the kitchen table shopping for curtains through home catalogs. Strawberry enters the kitchen. Apple and Cashew are playing outside.

Strawberry: Mom, why are the almonds in a jar of water in the fridge?

Amandine: I soaked these almonds overnight in preparation to make more almond milk, Strawberry.

Fig and Banana: Yea, more almond milk!

Strawberry: Why are you soaking the almonds first?

Amandine: Strawberry, there are many varieties of almonds and many ways to prepare them. I bought raw almonds for our recipe. In the raw, natural state, these almonds soaked in water can then sprout new life. Is it possible that soaking almonds also makes them easier to digest, increases the life force and nutrient content of the almonds, and allows the body to use the nutrients better than when the almonds haven't been soaked?

Fig: Yes, and by soaking the almonds first, we release the natural enzymes. Enzymes and optimal health & wellness go together. The enzymes in foods such as fruits, vegetables, nuts, and seeds eaten in their natural, uncooked states activate digestion.

Strawberry, Amandine, and Banana: Wow!

ACT THREE - SCENE 2

Amandine is in the kitchen. Fig is working on the computer in the living room. Banana is at the kitchen table shopping for curtains through home catalogs. Strawberry, Apple & Cashew enter the kitchen.

Apple: Mom, Dad, Nana! We're all invited to a community lunch potluck this weekend.

Strawberry: What do we bring?

Banana: Almond butter?

Fig: Almonds?

Cashew: More almond milk please!

Amandine: Almond milk. What a great idea! It's delicious & nutritious—a complement to water, juice, & soda.

Fig: Let's make & take almond milk.

Amandine: Hooray! Did you know in Jewish Culture almonds are a symbol of joy given to family & friends after Passover?*

Banana: Yes, indeed. Coconut and I will be at the potluck and I want to share the joy of almond milk with him too.

ACT THREE - SCENE 3

Fig, Apple, Strawberry & Cashew are in the kitchen. Banana and Amandine are at the kitchen table shopping for curtains through home catalogs.

Fig: The almond milk went fast at the community potluck yesterday.

Apple: Someone asked me if I like it.

Strawberry: Someone asked me if I drink it.

Amandine: Someone asked me if I make it.

Banana: And Coconut asked me if the two of us can make some together at home.

Cashew: I like almond milk!

Amandine: Me too! More almond milk please!

Fig: Oh, but we're out of almonds.

Banana: Try using some almond butter. Two tablespoons in one cup of water, with a banana, some cinnamon, sea salt...it's delightful and delicious!

Everyone: It's time for an almond milk smoothie!

THE END

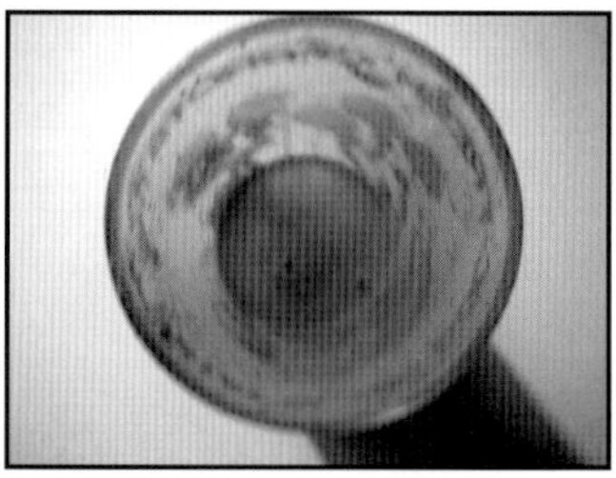

SOURCES

Books

Campbell, T. Colin, PHD with Campbell II, Thomas M. *The China Study.* Dallas, Texas: Benbella Books, 2005.

Cohen, Robert. *Milk A-Z.* Englewood Cliffs, NJ: Argus Publishing, 2001.

Cousens, Gabriel, M.D. *Spiritual Nutrition.* Berkeley, California: North Atlantic Books, 2005.

Robbins, John. *Healthy at 100.* New York: Random House, 2006.

Wigmore, Ann and Pattinson, Lee. *The Blending Book.* New York: Avery, 1997.

Yaron, Ruth. *Super Baby Food.* Archbald, PA: F. J. Roberts Publishing Company, 1998.

> I've had this book since December 1999 with a note I recorded in it—"Calvin's first food 1/28/00, ripe avocado". I have collected so much wisdom from this book during the past 7 years. I started preparing fresh nut/seed milks at home from the recipes listed under "Super Milks".

Natural Food Stores

Ask for stores in your local area.

People, Places, & Websites

Victoria, Igor, Sergei, & Valya Boutenko
WWW.RAWFAMILY.COM

> I appreciate particularly the Boutenko's family inspirational transformation, and Victoria's insights, valuable research, seminars, and books in the field of raw foods and healing, as well as the way "green smoothies" have revolutionized her life as almond milk has mine.

Gabriel Cousens, M.D.
WWW.TREEOFLIFE.NU

> I have experienced Gabriel Cousens as an exceptional doctor, healer, teacher, author, spiritual guide, speaker, leader, visionary and fellow community member through involvement with the Tree of Life Rejuvenation Center and Community.

Nick Good
WWW.SUCCESSULTRANOW.COM

Our family has experienced amazing inspiration, motivation, and transformation since early 2006 through Nick's coaching, business collaboration, friendship, neighboring, and programs, most especially for Chris and me, the 21-day SUN POP Guided Inner Journey.

Arnold Kauffman
WWW.ARNOLDSWAY.COM

Our family met Arnold during visits to his Lansdale, PA store during the last few years. It is a fun, delightful, and energizing place. Among his company, food, and health products, we recommend his artistic music CD *Can't Make a Mistake*.

Karen Knowler
WWW.KARENKNOWLER.TYPEPAD.COM
WWW.FRESH-NETWORK.COM

I have had the pleasure to experience Karen's effective coaching services com bined with her raw food knowledge.

Dr. Joseph Mercola
WWW.MERCOLA.COM

Dr. Mercola offers insightful natural health information and newsletter on this website.

Dhrumil Purohit
WWW.WELIKEITRAW.COM

Our family met Dhrumil, a friend of many like paths in Delaware. His blog is unique, humorous, and educational with regards to raw food.

Jinjee & Storm Talifero & Children
WWW.THEGARDENDIET.COM

Our family benefits greatly from the wisdom Jinjee and Storm impart in nurturing their growing family. They use cutting edge technology and media in raising consciousness worldwide and sharing their message of wellness.

David Wolfe
WWW.DAVIDWOLFE.COM
WWW.SUNFOOD.COM
WWW.THEBESTDAYEVER.COM

Chris and I met David for the first time in 2003 during one of his inspirational lectures in Delaware. He is well-versed in the transforming connection between the raw foods and wellness, a model for planetary healing, an accomplished writer, business associate, and friend.

Products & Organizations

The Almond Board of California
1150 Ninth Street, Suite 1500
Modesto, CA 95354
Phone: (209) 549-8262
WWW.ALMONDSAREIN.COM
WWW.ALMONDBOARD.COM

> I credit this group for facts* in the Play.

Tree of Life Rejuvenation Center
Patagonia, AZ
Phone: (520) 394-2520 & (866) 394-2520
WWW.TREEOFLIFE.NU

> Our family is grateful for numerous opportunities here, including educational workshops and lectures, being in Nature and connecting with Earth through gardening, healing treatments and live foods nutrition, medical consultation, spiritual growth and relationships with fellow community members, continued studies, yoga and more.

Natural Zing
P.O. Box 749
Mount Airy, MD 21771
Phone: (301) 703-4116 & (888) 729-9464
WWW.NATURALZING.COM

> Leaders in the wellness revolution and an amazing influence for a healthy East Coast USA, Jeff and Helen Rose attended and supported a local raw, organic chocolate party Chris and I hosted in Maryland in July, 2005. They specialize in natural, organic, vegan foods and live food community events.

Nature's First Law, Inc. / Sunfood Nutrition
11653 Riverside Drive
Lakeside, CA 92040
Phone: (619) 5956-7979 & (800) 205-2350 or (888) RAW-FOOD
WWW.RAWFOOD.COM
WWW.SUNFOOD.COM

> Since early 2003, Chris and I have bought high quality books, appliances, foods, and more from this company.

Sun Organic Farm
Box 409
San Marcos, CA 92079
Phone: (888) 269-9888
WWW.SUNORGANIC.COM

> I have bought many quality products from this company, and particularly like their selection of dried fruits and bulk nuts and seeds with which I make nut and seed milks.

TIPS FOR MAKING GREAT HOMEMADE RAW ORGANIC ALMOND MILK

- Use raw, organic, pesticide-free almonds.
- Soak almonds first.
- Invest in a nut milk bag.
- Involve children and company in the creation.
- Be happy: "whistle while you work."
- Fill the blender enough to prevent overflowing.
- Blend almonds well for a smooth consistency.
- Strain milk in small batches at a time.
- Be patient with initial efforts.
- Play with new spices, seasonings, and sweeteners.
- Make it everyday.
- Honor it as nourishing, life-giving food.
- Chill it in the refrigerator.
- Drink it within 2-3 days.

ACKNOWLEDGMENTS

For Bette-Lynne Rheinhardt, my mom: Thank you for providing me with a strong sense of family and devotion to homemaking and for instilling in me an appreciation for reading books and being an educated person in the world.

For Richard Svehla, my dad: Thank you for helping me see humor and divinity in everything and for celebrating me always.

For Megan Svehla, my sister: Thank you for giving me the experience of "big sister: and for your sweet beauty and social graces which warmly influence me and everyone in your presence.

For Jen Cassidy and April Coburn, my soul sisters: Thank you for traveling the conscious path with me. You always amaze me!

For Amy Pumphrey, Jessica Rhoten, Janine Meadows, Elizabeth Bidwell, and Sandy Larson, my friends: Thank you for blessing me with your friendship – all of you from different episodes of my life and equally as special.

For Kathy and Gooch Goodwin, our neighbors: Thank you for awakening my artistic talent, for your small town friendly hospitality, and for serving as my unofficial book publishing resources.

For everyone who has tasted my almond milk recipe, listened to our story, and passed the magic to another; and for you I have yet to encounter: I am especially grateful as you keep my fire burning and my visions alive and clear!

I also wish to acknowledge the special people in my life who have reviewed, edited, and encouraged The Almond Milk Book: Michela Casey, Jen Cassidy, April Coburn, Melissa Cox, Bette-Lynne Rheinhardt, and Jinjee Talifero. Thank you!

ABOUT THE AUTHOR

I completed my Bachelor of Nursing degree at the University of Delaware and Master of Science in Psychiatric Nursing degree at the University of Pennsylvania. My duties as a registered nurse included administering a lot of prescribed medication to people, who often resisted taking their medications or seemed to me to experience more symptoms related to taking so many medications. I have been inspired to write this book based on my personal health experiences, nursing career, and parenting responsibilities. Over the past 9 years of marriage and family living, I have refined my professional and instinctive nursing and holistic skills at home with my husband Chris and our children Calvin (7), Cosette (5), and Kurt (3), with almond milk included in our family's repertoire for wellness.

I enjoy simple pleasures such as sunshine, warm weather, baseball, family hikes, hugs, smiles, and dish fairies. I like to run, jump, play, cut, paste, color, draw, construct, and read books. My kitchen has a steady supply of almonds, not only for milk, but for snacks, salads, and sweets as well. I envision the day when almond milk is an available option to school children worldwide.

Married to a technically savvy husband, who has shared much of his computer wisdom with me over the years, I have discovered the wonders of the internet, including website development and the age of information. I have learned to create websites while "testing" Chris' work. He, too, has tested my work with plentiful samples of our family's almond milk.

You can contact me through the website:
WWW.THEALMONDMILKBOOK.COM

Additional Recipes & Notes